this book belongs to...

me —
cmartinez

EXTRAORDINARY TALES

EXTRAORDINARY TALES

JORGE LUIS BORGES
ADOLFO BIOY CASARES

Edited and Translated
With a Foreword by
ANTHONY KERRIGAN

A CONDOR BOOK
SOUVENIR PRESS (EDUCATIONAL & ACADEMIC) LTD

First British Edition published 1973 by
Souvenir Press (Educational & Academic) Ltd,
95 Mortimer Street, London W.1

ISBN 0 285 64712 1

Printed in Great Britain by
Fletcher & Son Ltd, Norwich

CONTENTS

FOREWORD BY ANTHONY KERRIGAN   7

NOTE ON THE ORIGINAL TEXTS   16

PRELIMINARY NOTE   17

EXTRAORDINARY TALES   19

FOREWORD

The whole history of human thought is nothing but the play of an infinite number of small nightmares of great consequence, whereas in sleep we have great nightmares of very short, very slight consequence.
Valéry, "A Fond Note on Myth"

IN his own work, Jorge Luis Borges has practiced, among other offices, that of chronicler of insomnia and of its equally unsleeping counterpart, nightmare. The states of the insomnia that he notes have included poignant and lucid memory. His degrees of dreaming or waking nightmare have been characterized by prescient insight, by epiphany. (His epiphanies we understand in the sense in which Joyce employed the term, the larger sense of passages of revelation and vision: Stephen Dedalus aspired to *write* epiphanies, so that "When one reads these strange pages of one long gone one feels that one is at one with one who once . . ." In the present anthology we have a type of such a dreamed-of book.) Borges' own obsession with a dream state—in the individual, in the created (or dreamt) world, in the gods or God—has forced his hand when writing, so that he writes of dreams which must be dreamt in the future, of man's fates which were dreamt in the past. And so we find that "the memory of the future" is of exactly the same potential as "the hope in the past" (Miguel de Unamuno's terms, but Unamuno

7

adumbrated Borges). And so we have here an anthology of, among other things, Remembrance of Things to Come (as in "The Return of the Master").

And Borges has wondered in writing if he—both of him—was in the past dreamt or is now being dreamed.

As regards the "consequence" of these dreams, we may ask: is, for instance, the opening piece in the present collection—a Chinese "Death Sentence" wherein a dragon is dreamt to death—a small nightmare of "great consequence," as our epigraph has it, or a great one of "very slight consequence"? Either way, it is worth repeating.

From the time of his first, particular, sense of the infinite, Borges has apparently suspected that everything has been dreamt before. He offers constant proof of this suspicion. His anthology of suspicions-previous-to-his-own is before us.

Borges and Bioy Casares have given us an anthology of "nightmares of great consequence" and of sheer moments of blinding insomniac consequence/inconsequence.

The anthology is also one of key metaphors, retrospective prophecies (Borges' "prophetic memory"), negative and positive adumbrations. In a cyclical way they duplicate each other, have been duplicated before, and Borges and Bioy enthusiastically encounter them in their reading and repeat them for us—here and in their work.

Their anthology is also (to multiply its description) consti-tuted of minuscule but deceptively consequential encounters, metempsychoses of further import, metaphysical equivocations, megalomaniacal cartographies (a map is drawn up exactly as large as the terrain it represents, to match every contour in size); of labyrinths, and anti-labyrinths (the Arabian desert). It is

8

also an anthology of orthodoxies, of heterodoxies before they turn into orthodoxies, or heresies which have died away but still live—somewhere. We read of the last witnesses of surpassed religions; of the cruel birth of new religions: a superimposed calligraphy of palimpsest religions. A phrase or a descriptive passage presents us with the subtle and superior logic of illogical faith; with an intuition only later to be believed—momentarily. (A short excerpt from Poe, a cross-sectional page, displays an extraterrestrial—"zero gravity"—sense not found or confirmed until vaccine experiments aboard Apollo–14.)

We have, then, an anthology of beliefs and their pantomimic or mimetic refutation. And it is an anthology of alien devils, house devils, one's own devils. For "Behind every rich man stands a devil, and behind every poor man stand two," as the Swiss folk proverb (quoted by Jung) has it. Temptation is everywhere (heretical, in "The Egyptian Temptation"; while in "The Cook," by Max Jacob, the Devil needs to cook only four dinners to bring his mum "masters" to talk of accepted religion and thus put them on the path to perdition).

An anthology of temptations, then, to be accepted or rejected. An anthology of epiphanies (Kafka's "Four Reflections" and many others). And an anthology of metaphors. An anthology of telepathies. An anthology of metempsychoses. An anthology of mistaken identity ("The Hidden Deer," "The Mendicant of Naples"), and of the "identity of (double) identification" ("The Encounter"), and of transposed long-distance identity ("The Return of the Master," "The Face of Death") and of equivocal identity (the famous "Dream of Chuang Tzu," Kafka's "The Truth About Sancho Panza").

Borges' work itself, which follows from these previous epiphanies and metaphors, is in large part a restatement of these particular epiphanies and metaphors, a fugal variation, or more precisely, *fugato* compositions.

Borges repeats (and here it is reiterated in this pre-summing-up, or Foreword which could as well be an Afterword) that our insights are repetitive.

But not to repeat can be cowardly. To shy away from re-doing what has already been done is, for Louis MacNeice, the primal sin:

> Never to begin
> Anything new because we know there is nothing
> New, is an academic sophistry—
> The original sin.

We read a contemporary manifesto from a literary group of High Standing, and quote: "The Greek myths bore; Christ on his cross bores; Marx bores; Lenin is getting to be boring; Mao will be boring." We demur: the Greek myths never were boring, certainly not from the start, nor was Christ, most especially not when hung from the Cross. The others were boring from the first—and therein lies the difference. (Though perhaps one should not use—even of those hopelessly repetitive Marxists who never repeated the basic myths, but only the raw new myths of their own *gauche* carpentry—one should probably not use the boring adjective "boring," even of them.) Significantly, Trotsky is not said to bore: for Trotsky was never *boring,* not from the London days in his teens through the days he was head of the 1905 St. Petersburg Soviet in his twenties until the days he collected cactus in Mexico.

It is whatever is epically repetitive which must be repeated, as the metempsychoses and myths collected here (and, like that which belongs to us all: the themes of, say, the Collective Unconscious, to give it a name). Robin Skelton puts the case for repetition plain:

> Each man must turn
> what is into what is,
> or he will die.

In the present summation of "narratives," even Death does not die, not even when death is a dream.

Lucretius, more Borgesian than Borges, contended that his lyric accounts in natural history were all true in some universe (there were so many!) or other. If the detailed narratives were not applicable in this cosmos, perhaps they belonged to the story of some other place. Borges, a universal historian himself, finds the infinite universe about us universe enough as to infinite possibilities; even its negative possibilities are infinite: nihilism itself is various. In our anthology we are served with cardinal passages which describe the whole of the conscious universe by describing a part, *ex ungue leonem,* a lion by its claw. Since a lion has fleas, Borges and Bioy also furnish us some flea-patches of prose ("Retrospective") to complement the claw and more fully describe the beast.

Borges, the subtlest of historians, understands that history is not *merely* a nightmare (not just a nightmare from which we are struggling to awake, as in Joyce's cosmology, but perhaps also a nightmare we are preparing to dream?); it is also a sequence of vividly insomniac epiphanies to be repeatedly relived. In these states of pre-nightmare the personae of the action step to the music of others as well as their own, inhabit the dreams of others as well as their own, are duplicated as brothers, antagonists (second actors), chance counters of a dream lottery. Borges

11

suspects a cyclical nihilism in it all, an annihilating repetition, a repetitious similitude, a simulacrum.

Borges' discovery elsewhere that Shakespeare was the sum of everyman—and therefore himself a no-man, nobody—is a spectacular find. Keats had hailed Shakespeare as a *"Negative Capability,* that is . . . a man . . . capable of being in uncertainties, mysteries, doubts, without any irritable reaching after fact and reason."* Borges seems to suggest that Shakespeare is a confluence of historic non-sequiturs, a Nobody, or better, a Nothing, perhaps clearest in his meaning only to a non-Englishman like Unamuno, who felt that Shakespeare was a creation of Hamlet *et al.,* or to a half-blind Argentine on the edge of the annihilating *pampa.* Other discoveries available to Borges include the epic importance of a verbal play involving non-revelation of their identity by two brothers—a pretender and a King—engaged in civil war in England ("The King's Promise"). In his essay on the "Modesty of History," he hails the "savor of heroism" in the odor of lavender, "ranker than the smell of horses and courage."

Borges is a crypto-classic. And the secret (*kruptos*) of his classicism is in the texts, and they in themselves are cryptic, which, as well as secret, means concise, laconic, succinct. His shorthand serves in making *précis* of numberless mythologies, personal as well as popular. In expounding his own unique vision, he establishes a valid syncretism of his own for uniting synopses of antique plots which have classically repeated each other. Previous tellers of antique tales, "synopsizers" of antique plots, seem less excruciatingly aware that they are retelling the eternal tales, re-synopsizing the plots. Few tellers could have been as interested in synopses (the original Spanish title includes the word *breve,* brief: *Cuentos breves* . . .). Borges is so aware that he is summing-up that he finds it natural to reproduce some of the previous synopses for us so that we may marvel in comparing the "Extraordinary."

In our anthology of "brief and extraordinary tales," most of the pieces are not tales so much as suggestive passages of para-Kabbalistic meaning: not the Kabbalistic theory of language, but a theory of key passages: not Word/World, but Sentence/Judgment. As it is for the Kabbalist, history here is a symbolic *repetition* in every man's soul. The Egyptian exodus was not once, but daily: in everyman a daily exodus from his own Egypt. The process of history is forestalled, anticipated in the past. Procession and reversion constitute a single moment.

Necessarily, too, the "tales" are classic: not popular classics, even if by nature classics must sooner or later be popular, but secret classics, crypto-classics re-visualized by the Argentine seer whose Buenos Aires of the mind is Paris Dublin Valldemosa, even, perhaps, an absurd Lourdes.

Any anthology must be a summation of non-sequiturs. That might be a weakness. But with the proper attitude, a collection of the world's non-sequiturs can be genial, in all principal senses of the word. "Gentlemen, it's Spring! Shall we redeem a legend?" Or a heresy? All the legends can be redeemed, all the sects re-deemed—most especially after the iconoclasts have wreaked their counter-believer's fury upon them—the only suspicion being that they have all been redeemed before, and that only *we* remain, meanwhile, as inexplicable as ciphers.

There is bound to be a curious repetitiveness to an anthology. (In Henry James' "The Pattern on the Carpet" here glossed by Arthur Machen there is found to be "one theme . . . in a whole shelf of books.")

13

There is also a curious duplication, doubleness, duplicity even. In the Borges-Bioy anthology of tales, a species of duplicity—double duplicity—is to be found in the two versions of "The Ubiquitous One." The first "tale" concerns the Buddha, walking along under the sun protected by such a multitude of sunshades that he multiplies the number of Buddhas to put one under each sunshade, thus accommodating the gods who provided such numerous sunshades; in the second "tale," a Hindustani god, importuned by a lustful fellow-god, extends his own sexual prowess, extends *himself* 14,515 times in order to satisfy 14,516 wives, and thus keep the other god from adulterous use of any one of all these wives. Double examples of long-distance identification-magic are to be found in Martin Buber's Rabbinical "Oversight" and in the Chinese "Sect of the White Lotus." And a game of chess decides a battle in Wales and another game decides another battle in Madagascar.

Borges' concern with the Great Duplicator—the Mirror—is well known. We are presented here with a tale ("Nosce Te Ipsum": Know Thyself) which might be called The Morality of the Mirror. For in it each man entering besieged Khartum is brought before the final court of a Mirror, an ethical court of self-vision, where he can, as it were, judge *himself* in and to his face by way of Final Judgment.

Geographically, the epiphanies and metaphors are European, Levantine, Near Eastern, Far Eastern, North and South American; Christian, Jewish, Hindu, Buddhist. (Despite the necromancy, nothing Negro seems to have been found: there is the one African item, the chess game to decide a battle, but out of Malay Madagascar.)

We are the time that is left us: but also the time that was

(*Time is. Time was. Time is past.*). And all the time to come?

We change each day. In his own work, Borges has shown us that we change each moment in regard to a mirror, the moon, a door, a book. And, parenthetically, we are always "practicing" time.

Within a parenthesis of his own, Borges writes: "(To arrange a library is to practice, in a quiet and modest way, the art of criticism.)." And Borges, aided by Bioy, gives us his "criticism" by arranging for us a library of reiterative passages—passages which he will, many of them, iterate and reiterate elsewhere, sooner or later.

ANTHONY KERRIGAN

Palma de Mallorca, 1971

NOTE ON THE ORIGINAL TEXTS

OF the 92 excerpts from various languages which follow, a goodly number were originally in English. Most of the original texts (all the important ones) were located, and we give them here in the exact words in which they were written in English. A few of the more unusual originals (the *Indian Antiquary,* some rare Richard Burton, short passages of exotica, certain China tiles and Orientalia, and such far-fetched works as *Rambling Thoughts on World History,* Niagara Falls, 1903) were not found. Even when the rarer Burton *was* located, the passages in question were not found and thus the exact wording by that author could not be given: there is good reason to believe that the translation into Spanish by the Argentine editors was idiosyncratic in the first place; in most cases, the translations into Spanish were found to have been freely compressed.

Special thanks for the location of texts are due Robert Kempner, the University of Arizona Library; to Miss Cora Pollock, the British Institute Library, Madrid; and to Kenneth Dolan, National College of Art, Dublin.

PRELIMINARY NOTE

ONE of the many pleasures which literature has to offer is that of the narrative. This book will endeavor to lay before the reader some examples of the *genre:* some of them imaginary happenings, some historical events. For our purpose, we have interrogated the texts of various nations and varied epochs, without neglecting the ancient and generous sources of the East. The anecdote, the parable, and the narrative have all been welcome, on the condition that they be brief.

The essence of narrative is to be found, we venture to think, in the present pieces; the rest is episodic illustration, psychological analysis, fortunate or inopportune verbal adornment. We trust, reader, that these pages will amuse you as they have amused us.

JORGE LUIS BORGES
ADOLFO BIOY CASARES

EXTRAORDINARY TALES

THE DEATH SENTENCE

THAT night, at the Hour of the Rat, the Emperor dreamt that he had walked out of the palace and in the darkness strolled through the garden, under the flowering trees. Something knelt at his feet and asked for asylum. The Emperor granted the favor; the supplicant said that he was a dragon and added that the stars had revealed to him that on the next day, before nightfall, Wei Cheng, the Emperor's Minister, would cut off his head. In the dream, the Emperor swore to protect him.

On waking, the Emperor asked after Wei Cheng. He was told that Wei Cheng was not in the palace. The Emperor sent for him, and then kept him busy the whole day through, so that the Minister might not kill the dragon; toward nightfall he proposed they play a game of chess. The game was long drawn out: the Minister grew weary, and fell asleep.

A clap of thunder shook the earth. Two captains presently burst upon the scene: they carried the immense head of a dragon drenched in blood. They threw it at the feet of the Emperor and vociferated: "It fell from the sky."

Wei Cheng, who had meanwhile awakened, gazed at the head in perplexity and observed: "How strange. I was dreaming I killed a dragon like that."

Wu Ch'eng-en (c. 1505–c. 1580)

21

THE SECRET REDEEMER

IT is well known that all ogres live in Ceylon and that all their beings are contained in a single lemon. A blind man slices the lemon and all the ogres die.

From the Indian Antiquary, I (1872)

THE ANNIHILATION OF THE OGRES

THE life of an entire tribe of ogres may be concentrated in two bees. The secret was revealed by an ogre to a captive princess, who pretended to fear that her ogre might not be immortal. "We ogres do not die," her ogre told her, so as to set her mind at rest. "We are not immortal, but our death depends upon a secret which no human will ever guess. I will reveal it to you to keep you from further suffering. Look here in this pond: in the middle, in the deepest part, there is a glass pillar on top of which, under water, two bees have settled. If a man were able to go under water and bring the two bees back to land and free them, all we ogres would die. But who would ever guess the secret? Don't worry, you can consider me immortal."

The princess revealed the secret to the hero. And he freed the bees and all the ogres died, each one in his own palace.

From *Folk Tales of Bengal* (London, 1883), by Lal Behari Day

THE STORY OF CECILIA

I HEARD Lucius Flaccus, high priest of Mars, tell the following story: Cecilia, daughter of Metellus, wanted to marry off the daughter of her sister and, in accord with the ancient custom, the two women repaired to a temple in search of some omen. The girl remained standing while Cecilia was seated; a long time elapsed without a single word being heard. The niece grew weary and said to Cecilia: "Allow me to sit a moment." "Of course, my dear," Cecilia said, "pray take my place."

These words constituted the omen, for Cecilia presently died and the niece married the widower.

Cicero, *De divinatione,* I, 46

THE ENCOUNTER

CH'IENNIANG was the daughter of Chang Yi, a public official in Hunan province. She had a cousin named Wang Chu, an intelligent and handsome youth. The two cousins had grown up together and, since Chang Yi both loved and approved of the boy, he said he would accept Wang Chu as his son-in-law. Both the young people heard and marked the promise; she was an only child and spent all her time with her cousin; their love grew day by day. And the day came when they were no longer children and their relations grew intimate. Unfortunately, her father, Chang Yi, was the only person around who did not notice. One day a young public official asked Chang Yi for his daughter's hand. The father, heedless or forgetful of his earlier promise, consented. Ch'ienniang, torn between love and filial piety, nearly died of grief; the young man fell into such despair that he resolved to leave the district rather than watch his mistress married to another man. He invented some pretext or other and told his uncle that he must go to the capital. When the uncle was unable to dissuade him, he supplied the youth with funds along with some presents and offered him a farewell banquet. In a desperate state, Wang Chu did not leave off moaning throughout the feast and was more than ever determined to go away rather than persist in a hopeless love affair.

The youth embarked one afternoon; he had sailed only a few miles when night fell. He ordered his sailor to tie up so that they might rest. But Wang Chu could not fall asleep; some time around midnight he heard footsteps approaching. He got up and called out: "Who is it, walking about at this hour of the night?" "I, Ch'ienniang," came the reply. Surprised and overjoyed he brought her aboard. She told him that she had hoped and expected to be his wife, that her father had been unjust, and that she could not resign herself to their separation. She had also feared that, finding himself alone in a strange land, he might have been driven to suicide. And so she had defied general disapproval and parental wrath and had now come to follow him wherever he might go. The happily re-united pair thereupon continued the journey on to Szechwan.

Five years of happiness passed, and she bore Wang Chu two children. But there was no news of Ch'ienniang's family and every day she thought of her father. It was the only cloud in their happy sky. She did not know whether or not her parents were still alive; and one night she confessed her anxiety to Wang Chu. Because she was an only daughter she felt guilty of a grave filial impiety. "You have the heart of a good daughter and I will stand by you," Wang Chu told her. "Five years have passed and they will no longer be angry with us. Let us go home." Ch'ienniang rejoiced and they made ready to go back with their children.

When the ship reached their native city, Wang Chu told Ch'ienniang: "We cannot tell in what state of mind we will find your parents. Let me go on alone to find out." At sight of the house, he could feel his heart pounding. Wang Chu saw his father-in-law, knelt down, made his obeisance, and begged his pardon. Chang Yi gazed upon him with amazement and said: "What are you talking about? For the past five years, Ch'ienniang has been lying in bed, in a coma. She has not gotten up once."

"But I have told you the truth," said Wang Chu. "She is well, and awaits us on board the ship."

Chang Yi did not know what to think and sent two maids-in-waiting to see Ch'ienniang. They found her seated aboard ship, beautifully gowned and radiant; she asked them to convey her fondest greetings to her parents. Struck with wonder, the maids-in-waiting returned to the parental house, where Chang Yi's bewilderment increased. Meanwhile, the sick girl had heard the news, and now seemed freed of her ill. There was a new light in her eyes. She rose from her bed and dressed in front of her mirror. Smiling and without a word, she made her way towards the ship. At the same time, the girl on the ship began walking toward the house. The two met on the river-bank. There they embraced and the two bodies merged, so that only one Ch'ienniang remained, as youthful and lovely as ever. Her parents were overjoyed, but they ordered the servants to keep quiet, to avoid commentaries.

For more than forty years Wang Chu and Ch'ienniang lived together in happiness.

A tale from the T'ang Dynasty (618–906 A.D.)

HARD TO PLEASE

KARDAN fell ill. His uncle asked him:
"What would you like to eat?"
"The head of two lambs."
"There isn't any."
"In that case, the two heads of a lamb."
"There aren't any."
"Then I don't want anything."

Ibn Abd Rabbith, *Kitabal idq el farid,* III

SCATTERED THEMES FROM
THE NOTE-BOOKS
OF NATHANIEL HAWTHORNE

A PERSON, while awake and in the business of life, to think highly of another, and place perfect confidence in him, but to be troubled with dreams in which this seeming friend appears to act the part of a most deadly enemy. Finally it is discovered that the dream character is the true one. The explanation would be—the soul's instinctive perception.

The situation of a man in the midst of a crowd, yet as completely in the power of another, life and all, as if they two were in the deepest solitude.

Some man of powerful character to command a person, morally subjected to him, to perform some act. The commanding person to suddenly die; and, for all the rest of his life, the subjected one continues to perform that act.

A rich man left by will his mansion and estate to a poor couple. They remove into it, and find there a darksome servant, whom they are forbidden by will to turn away. He becomes a torment to them; and, in the finale, he turns out to be the former master of the estate.

Two persons to be expecting some occurrence, and watching for the two principal actors in it, and to find that the occurrence is even then passing, and that they themselves are the two actors.

A person to be writing a tale, and to find that it shapes itself against his intentions; that the characters act otherwise than he thought; that unforeseen events occur; and a catastrophe comes which he strives in vain to avert. It might shadow forth his own fate—he having made himself one of the personages.

Nathaniel Hawthorne, *Note-Books* (1868)

THE DREAM OF CHUANG TZU

CHUANG Tzu dreamt he was a butterfly and, when he awoke, did not know if he was a man who had dreamt he was a butterfly or a butterfly who was dreaming he was a man.

From *Chuang Tzu* (1889),
by Herbert Allen Giles

THE HIDDEN DEER

A WOODCUTTER from Cheng found himself in a field with a frightened deer and slew it. To prevent others from finding it, he buried it in the woods, with a covering of leaves and branches. Only a short time later he forgot the hiding place and thought that he had dreamed the whole thing. He told everyone the story as if it had been a dream. Among his auditors was a man who went to look for the hidden deer and found it. He carried it home and told his wife:

"A woodcutter dreamt he had killed a deer, and then forgot where he hid it, and now I have found it. That woodcutter is indeed a dreamer."

"You have probably dreamt that you saw a woodcutter who had killed a deer. Do you really believe that there was such a woodcutter? Still, we have the deer in front of us, so your dream must be true," said the wife.

"Even assuming that I found the deer because of a dream," the husband retorted, "why bother to find out which of the two of us was dreaming?"

That night the woodcutter returned to his house, the deer still on his mind, and he really did dream, and in his dream he dreamt of the place where he had hidden the deer and also dreamt of the man who had found it. At dawn he went to the house of the other man and saw the deer. The two men argued, and ended up before a judge, to resolve the question. The judge addressed the woodcutter:

"You really killed a deer and thought it was a dream. Then you really dreamed and thought it was true. The other man found the deer and now he disputes it with you, but his wife thinks he dreamt he found a deer that someone else had killed. In short, no one killed a deer. But, since we have a deer before us here, the best course is to divide it between you."

The case reached the ears of the King of Cheng and the King of Cheng said:

"As for that judge, is he not dreaming that he is dividing a deer?"

Liehtse (c. 300 A.D.)

THE BRAHMINS AND THE LION

In a certain town lived four Brahmins who were friends. Three of them had achieved the limit of what men might know, but they lacked everyday wisdom. The fourth disdained knowledge; all he possessed was everyday wisdom. One day they met together. What good are natural endowments and talents, they asked one another, if we do not travel, if we do not gain the favor of kings, if we do not earn money? Before all else, let us travel.

But, then, when they had travelled a stretch, the elder said:

"One of us, the fourth, is a simpleton, who possesses only everyday wisdom. Without knowledge, and with mere everyday wisdom, no one may obtain the favor of kings. Therefore, let us not share our gains with him. Let him return home."

The second one said:

"My intelligent friend, you are lacking in wisdom. Go back home."

The third said:

"This is no way to carry on. We have played together since we were children. Come, my noble friend. You shall have a portion of our gains."

They continued on their way and, in a woods, they came upon the bones of a lion. One of the men spoke:

"This is a good opportunity to exercise our knowledge. Here is a dead animal: let us bring it back to life."

The first said:

"I know how to assemble the skeleton."

The second said:

"I can provide the skin, the flesh, and the blood."

The third said:

"I know how to give it life."

The first assembled the skeleton, the second provided the skin, the flesh, and the blood. The third got ready to imbue the creature with life, when the man of everyday wisdom observed:

"It is a lion. If you bring it back to life, it will kill us all."

"You are very simple-minded," said another. "I will not be the one to frustrate the workings of knowledge."

"In that case," replied the man of everyday wisdom, "wait a moment while I climb this tree."

When he had climbed the tree, the others brought the lion back to life. The lion rose up and killed the three of them. The man of everyday wisdom waited until the lion had gone away before descending from the tree and returning home.

Panchatantra (second century A.D.)

A GOLEM

If the Just wished to create a world, they could do so. By combining the letters of the ineffable names of God, the Talmudist Rava was able to create a man; he sent him to Rav Zera, who spoke to him; when the creature did not reply, the Rabbi told him: "You are a creation of magic; go back to your dust."

There were also two masters who studied the *Sefer Yetsirah,* the "Book of Creation," every Friday, and then created a three-year-old calf, which they thereupon used to good advantage for their supper.

Sanhedrin, 65, b.

THE RETURN OF THE MASTER

FROM his earliest years, Migyur—for such was his name—had always felt that *he was not where he should have been*. He felt himself a stranger to his family, a stranger in his village. In his dreams, he would behold landscapes not proper to Ngari: sand wastes, round felt tents, a monastery on a mountain; in his waking hours, these same images blurred reality, veiled it.

When he was nineteen he fled, eager to encounter the reality corresponding to these forms. He became a vagabond, a beggar, a workman, sometimes a thief. On this particular day he arrived at that inn, close by the frontier.

He saw the house, the weary Mongol caravan, the camels in the courtyard. He crossed the threshold and found himself before the ancient monk who commanded the caravan. It was then that they recognized each other: the young vagabond saw himself as an ancient lama and saw the lama, the monk as he had been many years ago, when the monk had been his disciple; the monk recognized his old master, now gone, in the boy. Together they recalled the peregrination they had made to the sanctuaries of Tibet, the return to the mountain monastery. They conversed together, evoked the past; they interrupted each other to furnish precise details.

The purpose of the Mongols' journey was to search for a new chief for their convent. It was twenty years since the old chief had died and for that length of time they had waited in vain for his re-incarnation. Today they had found him.

At dawn, the caravan began its slow trek back. Migyur was returning to the sand wastes, the round tents, and the mountain monastery of his previous incarnation.

Alexandra David-Neel, *Magic and Mystery in Tibet* (1929)

IN FEAR OF WRATH

In one of his wars, Ali felled his opponent and knelt on his chest to cut off his head. The man spit in his face. Ali stood up and let him go. When he was asked why he had done so, he replied:

"He spit in my face and I was fearful of killing him in a rage. I want to kill my enemies only when I am pure in the sight of God."

Ah'med el Qalyubi, *Nanadir*

ANDROMEDA

THE dragon was never in better health and spirits than on the morning when Perseus came down upon him. It is said that Andromeda told Perseus she had been thinking how remarkably well he was looking. He had got up quite in his usual health, etc. When I said this to Ballard . . . he said he wished it had been so in the poets. I looked at him and said that I too was "the poets."

Samuel Butler, *Note-Books*
(London, 1951)

THE DREAM

MURRAY dreamed a dream.

Both psychology and science grope when they would explain
to us the strange adventures of our immaterial selves when wandering in the realm of "Death's twin brother, sleep." This story
will not attempt to be illuminative; it is no more than a record
of Murray's dream. One of the most puzzling phases of that
strange waking sleep is that dreams which seem to cover months
or even years may take place within a few seconds or minutes.

Murray was waiting in his cell in the ward of the condemned.
An electric arc light in the ceiling of the corridor shone brightly
upon his table. On a sheet of white paper an ant crawled wildly
here and there as Murray blocked its way with an envelope. The
electrocution was set for eight o'clock in the evening. Murray
smiled at the antics of the wisest of insects.

There were seven other condemned men in the chamber. Since
he had been there Murray had seen three taken out to their fate;
one gone mad and fighting like a wolf caught in a trap; one,
no less mad, offering up a sanctimonious lip-service to Heaven;
the third, a weakling, collapsed and strapped to a board. He wondered with what credit to himself his own heart, foot, and face
would meet his punishment; for this was his evening. He thought
it must be nearly eight o'clock.

Opposite his own in the two rows of cells was the cage of

Bonifacio, the Sicilian slayer of his betrothed and of two officers who came to arrest him. With him Murray had played checkers many a long hour, each calling his move to his unseen opponent across the corridor.

Bonifacio's great booming voice with its indestructible singing quality called out:

"Eh, Meestro Murray; how you feel—all-a right—yes?"

"All right, Bonifacio," said Murray steadily, as he allowed the ant to crawl upon the envelope and then dumped it gently on the stone floor.

"Dat's good-a, Meestro Murray. Men like us, we must-a die like-a men. My time come nex'-a week. All-a right. Remember, Meestro Murray, I beat-a you dat las' game of de check. Maybe we play again some-a time. I don'-a know. Maybe we have to call-a de move damn-a loud to play de check where dey goin' send us."

Bonifacio's hardened philosophy, followed closely by his deafening, musical peal of laughter, warmed rather than chilled Murray's numbed heart. Yet, Bonifacio had until next week to live.

The cell-dwellers heard the familiar, loud click of the steel bolts as the door at the end of the corridor was opened. Three men came to Murray's cell and unlocked it. Two were prison guards; the other was "Len"—no; that was in the old days; now the Reverend Leonard Winston, a friend and neighbor from their barefoot days.

"I got them to let me take the prison chaplain's place," he said, as he gave Murray's hand one short, strong grip. In his left hand he held a small Bible, with his forefinger marking a page.

Murray smiled slightly and arranged two or three books and

some penholders orderly on his small table. He would have spoken, but no appropriate words seemed to present themselves to his mind.

The prisoners had christened this cellhouse, eighty feet long, twenty-eight feet wide, Limbo Lane. The regular guard of Limbo Lane, an immense, rough, kindly man, drew a pint bottle of whiskey from his pocket and offered it to Murray saying:

"It's the regular thing, you know. All has it who feel like they need a bracer. No danger of it becoming a habit with 'em, you see."

Murray drank deep into the bottle.

"That's the boy!" said the guard. "Just a little nerve tonic, and everything goes smooth as silk."

They stepped into the corridor, and each one of the doomed seven knew. Limbo Lane is a world on the outside of the world; but it had learned, when deprived of one or more of the five senses, to make another sense supply the deficiency. Each one knew that it was nearly eight, and that Murray was to go to the chair at eight. There is also in the many Limbo Lanes an aristocracy of crime. The man who kills in the open, who beats his enemy or pursuer down, flushed by the primitive emotions and the ardor of combat, holds in contempt the human rat, the spider, and the snake.

So, of the seven condemned only three called their farewells to Murray as he marched down the corridor between the two guards—Bonifacio, Marvin, who had killed a guard while trying to escape from the prison, and Bassett, the train-robber, who was driven to it because the express-messenger wouldn't raise his hands when ordered to do so. The remaining four smoldered, silent, in their cells, no doubt feeling their social ostracism in Limbo Lane society more keenly than they did the memory of their less picturesque offenses against the law.

Murray wondered at his own calmness and nearly indifference. In the execution room were about twenty men, a congregation made up of prison officers, newspaper reporters, and lookers-on who had succeeded . . .

Here, in the very middle of a sentence, "The Dream" was interrupted by the death of O. Henry. Nevertheless we know the end: Murray, accused and convicted of the murder of his sweetheart, faces his destiny with inexplicable indifference. He is led to the electric chair, strapped in. Of a sudden, the death chamber, the spectators, the preparations for the execution, all seem unreal. It occurs to him that he is the victim of a frightful error. Why has he been strapped to this chair? What has he done? What crime has he committed? He awakes: his wife and child are beside him. He realizes that the murder, the trial, the death-sentence, the electric chair, are all a dream. Still trembling, he kisses his wife on the forehead. At that moment he is electrocuted. The execution interrupts Murray's dream.

O. Henry

THE KING'S PROMISE

TOSTIG—brother to the Saxon king of England, Harold, son of Godwin—coveted power and allied himself with Harald Sigurdsson, King of Norway. (The latter had campaigned in Byzantium and in Africa; his standard was called Landöda, Ravager of Lands; he was also a famous poet.) Tostig and Harald landed at the head of a Norwegian army on the east coast of England and reduced the fortress of Jorvik (York). South of Jorvik they were faced by the Saxon army. Twenty horsemen approached the invader's ranks; the horses as well as the men were covered in mail. One of the horsemen shouted:

"Is Earl Tostig there?"

"I don't deny being here," replied the Earl.

"If you really are Tostig," said the horseman, "I come to tell you that your brother offers you his pardon, his friendship, and a third part of the kingdom."

"If I accept," said Tostig, "what will the King give Harald Sigurdsson?"

"He has not forgotten him," answered the rider. "He will give him six feet of English earth and, since he is so tall, one more foot as well."

"Then tell your King," said Tostig, "that we will fight to the death."

The horsemen rode back. Harald Sigurdsson asked thoughtfully:

"Who was that man who spoke so well?"

"That was Harold, son of Godwin."

Before the sun set that day, the Norwegian army was destroyed. Harald Sigurdsson was slain in battle and so was the Earl.

Heimskringla, 91–92

THE CAPTIVE'S OATH

THE Jinni told the fisherman who had let him out of the jar of yellow copper:

"I am one of the heretical Jinni and I rose against Solomon, son of David (on the twain be peace!). I was defeated. Solomon, son of David, bade me embrace the Faith of God and obey his behests. I refused. The King shut me up in this copper recipient and impressed on the cover the Most High Name, and he ordered the submissive Jinni to cast me into the midmost of the ocean. I said in my heart: 'Whoso shall release me, him I shall make rich forever.' But an entire century passed, and no one set me free. Then I said in my heart: 'Whoso shall release me, to him shall I reveal all the magic arts of the earth.' But four hundred years passed and I remained at the bottom of the sea. Then I said: 'Whoso releases me, him will I give three wishes.' But nine hundred years passed. Then, in despair, I swore by the Most High Name: 'Whoever will set me free, him will I slay. Prepare to die, O my saviour!'"

From the Third Night of the Book of
The Thousand and One Nights

NOSCE TE IPSUM

THE Mahdi and his hordes were laying siege to Khartum, defended by General Gordon. A few of the enemy passed through the lines and entered the besieged city. Gordon received them one by one and indicated a mirror where they might see themselves. He thought it only right that a man should know his own face before he died.

Fergus Nicholson, Antología de espejos

THE INTUITIVE ONE

THEY say that in the center of Andalusia, in its kidney, so to speak, there was a school of medicine. The master asked:

"What's the position on this patient, Pepe, my boy?"

"As far as I can tell," replied the disciple, "he has got a cephalalgia between his chest and his back, and that's cooked his goose."

"And why do you say so, my salty fellow?"

"Master, because it comes from my soul, sir."

Alfonso Reyes, *El deslinde* (1944)

HOW I FOUND THE SUPERMAN

READERS of Mr. Bernard Shaw and other modern writers may be interested to know that the Superman has been found. I found him; he lives in South Croydon. My success will be a great blow to Mr. Shaw, who has been following quite a false scent, and is now looking for the creature in Blackpool; and as for Mr. Wells's notion of generating him out of gases in a private laboratory, I always thought it doomed to failure. I assure Mr. Wells that the Superman at Croydon was born in the ordinary way, though he himself, of course, is anything but ordinary.

Nor are his parents unworthy of the wonderful being whom they have given to the world. The name of Lady Hypatia Smythe-Browne (now Lady Hypatia Hagg) will never be forgotten in the East End, where she did such splendid social work. Her constant cry of "Save the children!" referred to the cruel neglect of children's eyesight involved in allowing them to play with crudely painted toys. She quoted unanswerable statistics to prove that children allowed to look at violet and vermilion often suffered from failing eyesight in their extreme old age; and it was owing to her ceaseless crusade that the pestilence of the Monkey-on-the-Stick was almost swept from Hoxton. The devoted worker would tramp the streets untiringly, taking away the toys from all the poor children, who were often moved to tears by her kindness. Her good work was interrupted, partly by a new interest in the creed of Zoroaster, and partly by a savage blow from an umbrella. It was inflicted by a dissolute Irish apple-woman, who, on returning from some orgy to her ill-kept apartment, found Lady Hypatia in the bedroom taking down an oleograph, which, to say the least of it, could not really elevate the mind. At this the ignorant and partly intoxicated Celt dealt the social reformer a severe blow, adding to it an absurd accusation of theft. The lady's exquisitely balanced mind received a shock, and it was during a short mental illness that she married Dr. Hagg.

Of Dr. Hagg himself I hope there is no need to speak. Any one even slightly acquainted with those daring experiments in Neo-Individualist Eugenics, which are now the one absorbing interest of the English democracy, must know his name and often commend it to the personal protection of an impersonal power. Early in life he brought to bear that ruthless insight into the history of religions which he had gained in boyhood as an electrical engineer. Later he became one of our greatest geologists; and achieved that bold and bright outlook upon the future Socialism which only geology can give. At first there seemed something like a rift, a faint, but perceptible, fissure, between his views and those of his aristocratic wife. For she was in favour (to use her own powerful epigram) of protecting the poor against themselves; while he declared pitilessly, in a new and striking metaphor, that the weakest must go to the wall. Eventually, however, the married pair perceived an essential union in the unmistakably modern character of both their views; and in this enlightening and intelligible formula their souls found peace. The result is that this union of the two highest types of our civilization, the fashionable lady and the all but vulgar medical man, has been blessed by the birth of the Superman, that being whom all the labourers in Battersea are so eagerly expecting night and day.

I found the house of Dr. and Lady Hypatia Hagg without much difficulty; it is situated in one of the last straggling streets of Croydon, and overlooked by a line of poplars. I reached the door towards the twilight, and it was natural that I should fancifully see something dark and monstrous in the dim bulk of that house which contained the creature who was more marvellous than the children of men. When I entered the house I was received with exquisite courtesy by Lady Hypatia and her husband; but I found much greater difficulty in actually seeing the Superman, who is now about fifteen years old, and is kept by himself in a quiet room. Even my conversation with the father and mother did not quite clear up the character of this mysterious being. Lady Hypatia, who has a pale and poignant face, and is clad in those impalpable and pathetic greys and greens with which she has brightened so many homes in Hoxton, did not appear to talk of her offspring with any of the vulgar vanity of an ordinary human mother. I took a bold step and asked if the Superman was nice looking.

"He creates his own standard, you see," she replied, with a slight sigh. "Upon that plane he is more than Apollo. Seen from our lower plane, of course—" And she sighed again.

I had a horrible impulse, and said suddenly, "Has he got any hair?"

There was a long and painful silence, and then Dr. Hagg said smoothly: "Everything upon that plane is different; what he has got is not . . . well, not, of course, what we call hair . . . but—"

"Don't you think," said his wife, very softly, "don't you think that really, for the sake of argument, when talking to the mere public, one might call it hair?"

"Perhaps you are right," said the doctor after a few moments' reflection. "In connection with hair like that one must speak in parables."

"Well, what on earth is it," I asked in some irritation, "if it isn't hair? Is it feathers?"

"Not feathers, as we understand feathers," answered Hagg in an awful voice.

I got up in some irritation. "Can I see him, at any rate?" I asked. "I am a journalist, and have no earthly motives except curiosity and personal vanity. I should like to say that I had shaken hands with the Superman."

The husband and wife had both got heavily to their feet, and stood, embarrassed.

"Well, of course, you know," said Lady Hypatia, with the really charming smile of the aristocratic hostess. "You know he can't exactly shake hands . . . not hands, you know . . . The structure, of course—"

I broke out of all social bounds, and rushed at the door of the room which I thought to contain an incredible creature. I burst it open; the room was pitch dark. But from in front of me came a small sad yelp, and from behind me a double shriek.

"You have done it, now!" cried Dr. Hagg, burying his bald brow in his hands. "You have let in a draught on him and he is dead."

As I walked away from Croydon that night I saw men in black carrying out a coffin that was not of any human shape. The wind wailed above me, whirling the poplars, so that they drooped and nodded like the plumes of some cosmic funeral. "It is, indeed," said Dr. Hagg, "the whole universe weeping over the frustration of its most magnificent birth." But I thought that there was a hoot of laughter in the high wail of the wind.

G. K. Chesterton

THE KING'S AWAKENING

FOLLOWING their military defeat in 1753, French agents in Canada spread the word among the Indians that the King of France had fallen into a deep slumber and had slept through the past few years, but that he had just now awakened and that his first words were: "We must immediately expel the English who have invaded the country of my red-skinned children." The word spread throughout the continent and was one of the causes of the famous conspiracy of Pontiac.

H. Desvignes Doolittle, *Rambling Thoughts on World History* (Niagara Falls, 1903)

DEATH OF A CHIEF

WHEN Cacharí's irregulars were defeated by the soldiery, Cacharí was left for dead on the banks of the lake which today bears his name. The local inhabitants tell of how for two days and two nights, in a mad frenzy, the dying chief howled as if he still wanted to fight: "Here's Cacharí, Cacharí, Cacharí . . ."

León Rivera, *Bocetos de un asistente*
(La Plata, 1894)

THE ANNOUNCEMENT

DURING one of the ancient wars of Scotland, the chief of the Douglas clan fell into enemy hands. The following day they brought to him, to his room in the tower, the head of a boar on a platter. As soon as he saw it, Douglas understood that his fate was sealed. That night he was beheaded.

George D. Brown, *Gleanings in Caledonian Byways* (Dunbar, 1901)

THE EXPLANATION

The implacable skeptic Wang Ch'ung denied the race of the phoenix. He declared that just as the serpent turns into a fish and the mouse into a turtle, so the stag is transformed, in times of peace and tranquility, into a unicorn, and the gander into a phoenix. He attributed these mutations to the "propitious liquid" which, 2356 years before the Christian era, caused the courtyard of the Emperor Yao to sprout grass the color of scarlet.

> Edwin Broster, *Addenda to a History of Freethinking*
> (Edinburgh, 1887)

AN ALEXANDRIAN MYTH

Who does not recall the poem by Robert Graves in which it is dreamt that Alexander the Great did not die in Babylon but that, having strayed away from his army and gotten lost, he penetrated ever deeper into Asia? After wandering about that unknown geography, he came upon an army of yellow men and, since his trade was warfare, he joined their ranks. Many years passed, and, on a certain pay day, Alexander gazed with some astonishment upon a gold coin which had been given him. He recognized the effigy and thought: I had this coin struck, to celebrate a victory over Darius, when I was Alexander of Macedon.

Adrienne Bordenave, *La modification du Passé ou la seule base de la Tradition* (Pau, 1949)

THE WORK AND THE POET

THE Hindu poet Tulsi Das composed the *Geste* of Hanuman
and his army of monkeys. Years later, he was imprisoned in a
stone tower by a king. In his cell he put himself to meditating,
and from out of his meditation emerged Hanuman and his
army of monkeys, and they conquered the city, burst into the
tower, and freed Tulsi Das.

R. F. Burton, *Indica* (1887)

EUGENICS

A LADY of quality fell so deliriously in love with a certain Mr. Dodd, a Puritan preacher, that she begged her husband to allow her to use the marital bed for purposes of procreating an angel or a saint; but, permission having been granted, the birth was normal.

Drummond, *Ben Ionsiana* (c. 1618)

THE MENDICANT OF NAPLES

WHEN I lived in Naples, there stood, at the door of my palace, a female mendicant to whom I used to pitch coins before mounting the coach. One day, suddenly perplexed at the fact that she never gave me any signal of thanks, I looked at her fixedly. It was then I saw that what I had taken for a mendicant was rather a wooden box, painted green, filled with red earth and some half-rotted banana peels.

Max Jacob, *Le Cornet à Dés* (1917)

A GOD ABANDONS ALEXANDRIA

THERE is a tale told of how when Antony at Alexandria was besieged by Caesar's troops and the city had fallen into the dazed silence of despair, in fearful expectation of what would happen, a vast sound gradually took shape: it was caused by the reverberation of numerous instruments and the tumult of a great mass of people indulging themselves in satyric songs and dances, like the passage of a frenzied rout of Bacchantes. This multitude was said to have set out from the center of the city and made its way toward the gate which led to the enemy camp; once it had passed through the gate, this vast joyous tumult evanesced. In the eyes of those who credit omens and portents, it was a sign to Antony that he was being abandoned by Bacchus, the god with whom he had always boasted a likeness, and in whom he had a singular faith.

From *The Parallel Lives of Plutarch*

THE FEMALE DISCIPLE

THE beautiful Hsi Shih knit her brows in a frown. A hideous peasant girl saw her and was struck dumb with wonder. She yearned to imitate the great lady; laboriously she put herself into a bad humor and knit her brows in annoyance. Then she went out into the street. The rich fled, locked themselves in their houses, and refused to come out; the poor loaded themselves down with their wives and children and set off for distant lands.

Herbert Allen Giles, *Chuang Tzu* (1889)

THE NINTH SLAVE

IBRAHIM, prince of Shirwan, or Albania, kissed the footstool of the Imperial throne. His peace-offerings of silks, horses, and jewels were composed, according to the Tartar fashion, each article of nine pieces; but a critical spectator observed that there were only eight slaves. "I myself am the ninth," replied Ibrahim, who was prepared for the remark, and his flattery was rewarded by the smile of Timour.

Gibbon, *Decline and Fall of the Roman Empire*, Chapter LXV

A VICTOR

A DIFFERENT sort of compassion was *seen* in Himilcon. Though he had achieved great victories in Sicily, he so mourned the loss of the many victims to illness in the army, that when he entered Carthage he did not do so in triumph, but dressed in mourning, draped in an open pilgrim's cloak—a slave's habit—and, on reaching his house, without saying a word to anyone, took his own life.

Saavedra Fajardo, *Idea de un Príncipe Político-cristiano,* XCVI (1640)

THE DANGEROUS WONDER-WORKER

A CLERIC who disbelieved in Mormonism went to visit Joseph Smith, the prophet, and asked him to work a miracle. Smith answered him:

"Very well, sir. I leave the choice to you. Would you perfer to be struck blind or deaf? Do you choose paralysis, or would you rather that your hand wither? Speak! And in the name of Jesus Christ I shall satisfy your desires."

The cleric stuttered that these were not the kind of miracles he had requested.

"In that case, sir," said Smith, "you shall remain without your miracle. I refuse to hurt other people merely to convince you."

M. R. Werner, *Brigham Young* (1925)

THE CASTLE

THUS he arrived before a great castle, on whose façade were carved the words: I BELONG TO NO ONE AND TO ALL. BEFORE ENTERING YOU WERE ALREADY HERE. WHEN YOU LEAVE YOU WILL REMAIN.

From *Jacques Le Fataliste* (1773), by Diderot

THE STATUE

THE statue of the goddess in Saïs bore the following enigmatic inscription: I AM ALL THAT HAS BEEN, ALL THAT IS, ALL THAT WILL BE, AND NO MORTAL (UP TO NOW) HAS RAISED MY VEIL.

From the ninth paragraph of the treatise
Of Isis and Osiris, by Plutarch

THE WARNING

IN the Canary Islands there stood an enormous bronze statue of a horseman who pointed with his sword towards the West. Engraved on the pedestal were the words: TURN BACK. BEHIND ME THERE IS NOTHING.

R. F. Burton, *1001 Nights,* II, 141

THE PROWESS OF VILLENA

A scant few years after the death of the Lord of Iniesta, the alchemists, and other illuminati or gulls, began to take possession of his name and to invent apocryphal books which they assigned to him or which they presumed to have found in his famous library. One of these works was the *Book of the Treasure,* or *of the Lock,* which, by means of an even greater falsehood, they sought to attribute to the glorious memory of Alfonso the Wise. But even more curious and significant in this connection is the *letter* which is alleged to have been written to Don Enrique de Villena by *the twenty wise men of Cordoba.* In this wondrous document Villena is granted, among other marvellous faculties, the prowess of being able to *ruddy* the sun by means of the *"heliotropia"* stone, to divine the future by means of the *"ohelonites,"* make himself invisible with the help of the herb *"andromena,"* make rain and lightning at will with the *"baxillo de arambre,"* and congeal air in spherical form with the aid of the herb *"yelopia."* Replying to his disciples, Don Enrique relates an allegorical dream in which Hermes Trismegistus, universal master of the sciences, mounted on a peacock, comes to bestow on him a plume and a table of geometric figures and the key to an enchanted palace, and, finally, the arc of the four keys, wherein is locked the great alchemical mystery.

From the *Antología de Poetas Líricos Castellanos,* Menéndez y Pelayo

THE SHADOW OF THE MOVES, I

IN one of the tales which make up the series of the *Mabinogion,*
two enemy kings play chess while in a nearby valley their
respective armies battle and destroy each other. Messengers ar-
rive with reports of the battle; the kings do not seem to hear
them and, bent over the silver chessboard, they move the gold
pieces. Gradually it becomes apparent that the vicissitudes of the
battle follow the vicissitudes of the game. Toward dusk, one of
the kings overturns the board because he has been checkmated,
and presently a blood-spattered horseman comes to tell him:
"Your army is in flight. You have lost the kingdom."

Edwin Morgan, *The Week-End Companion
to Wales and Cornwall* (Chester, 1929)

THE SHADOW OF THE MOVES, II

WHEN the French laid siege to the capital of Madagascar in 1893, the priests of the native religion participated in the defense by playing fanorona,* and the queen and people followed the moves of the game—ritually played to assure victory—with greater concern than they did the efforts of the troops.

Celestino Palomeque, *Cabotaje en Mozambique* (Porto Alegre, n. d.)

* A kind of chess.

THE CULPABLE EYES

THE tale goes that a man bought a girl for four thousand denarii. One day he gazed upon her, and burst into tears. The girl asked him why he wept. He answered: "You have such beautiful eyes that I forget to adore God." When she was left alone, the girl tore out her eyes. The man saw her then and was afflicted. "Why did you do violence to yourself? You have diminished your worth." She replied: "I do not wish anything in me to keep you from adoring God." That night, the man heard a voice in his dreams telling him: "The girl diminished her worth for you, but she increased it for us and we have taken her from you." On waking, he found four thousand denarii under his pillow. The girl was dead.

Ah'med ech Chiruani, *H'adiquat el Afrah*

THE PROPHET, THE BIRD, AND THE NET

IsRAELITE tradition tells the story of a prophet who encountered a net strung across his way; a bird nearby said to him: "Prophet of the Lord, in your life have you ever heard of a man so simple-minded as the one who hung this net to catch me, catch *me,* when I can see it?" The prophet went his way. On his return, he found the bird caught in the net. "How strange," he exclaimed. "Was it not you who a little while ago told me such and such?"

"Prophet," replied the bird, "when the appointed hour comes, we no longer have eyes nor ears."

Ah'med et Tortuchi, *Siradj el Moluk*

THE CELESTIAL DEER

THE *Tzu Puh Yü* relates that the celestial deer live in the depths of the mines. These fantastic animals desire to get to the surface and they seek the support of the miners to do so. They promise to lead the miners to veins of precious metals; when the stratagem fails, the deer harass the miners, and the latter finally must overpower them, immuring them in the galleries behind rocks cemented with clay. Sometimes the deer outnumber the miners and then they torture the latter and bring about their deaths.

The deer which manage to emerge into the light of day turn into a fetid liquid which spreads pestilence.

G. Willoughby-Meade, *Chinese Ghouls and Goblins* (1928)

THE COOK

THEY were as gluttonous as they were niggardly, the Lord and Lady. The first time the cook came in, cap in hand, saying, "May I ask if the Lord and Lady are well served?", they answered him, "We shall let you know through the butler." The second time they did not answer. The third time they thought of dismissing him, but could not make up their minds, for he was an exceptional cook. The fourth time (Good Lord! They lived in the outskirts, they were always alone, they got so bored), the fourth time they began: "The caper sauce, superb, but the partridge *canapé,* half-hard." They went on talking: of sports, of politics, of religion. Which was what the cook wanted, for he was none other than Fantomas, the tempter.

Max Jacob, *Le Cornet à Dés* (1917)

POLEMICISTS

VARIOUS gauchos in the general store are discussing writing and phonetics. Albarracín, from Santiago, cannot read or write, but he assumes that Cabrera is unaware of his illiteracy; Albarracín maintains that the word *trara** cannot be written. Crisanto Cabrera, also illiterate, holds that everything spoken can be written. "I will pay everybody's round," says Albarracín, "if you can write *trara*." "It is a bet," answers Cabrera; he takes out his knife and with its point scribbles something on the earth floor. From somewhere behind, old Álvarez leans over, stares at the floor, and pronounces judgment: "Clear as clear: *trara*."

> Luis L. Antuñano, *"Cincuenta años en Gorchs"*
> (*Medio siglo en campos de Buenos Aires,*
> Olavarría, 1911)

* *Trara:* iron tripod support for *mate* tea-kettle.

PERPLEXITIES OF THE COWARD

Revolt broke out in the army. A cuirassier flung himself upon his mount to saddle him, but, in the confusion, put the halter on the tail, and cried out to the horse: "Damned if your forehead hasn't gotten wider and your mane gotten longer!"

Ah'med el Ibelichi, *Mostatref*

THE RESTITUTION OF THE KEYS

When the Roman legions occupied the city of Jerusalem, the High Priest, who knew he would perish by the sword, wished to restore the keys of the sanctuary to the Lord. He threw them to heaven, and the hand of the Lord took them. All this had already been prophesied in the Apocalypse of Baruch.

From the treatise *Taanith,* of the Mishnah, Ch. XXIX

TRAINED SEPULCHRES

In Hyrcania, the plebs feed public dogs; the great and the noble feed domestic dogs. As you well know, those lands produce the best breeds of dogs. And these dogs are raised by each according to his abilities, so that when the animals die they may be devoured, which the natives believe to be the best form of sepulture.

From *Tusculanae Disputationes,*
by Marcus Tullius Cicero, Bk. 1

THE SILENCE OF THE SIRENS

PROOF that inadequate, even childish measures, may serve to rescue one from peril.

To protect himself from the Sirens Ulysses stopped his ears with wax and had himself bound to the mast of his ship. Naturally any and every traveller before him could have done the same, except those whom the Sirens allured even from a great distance; but it was known to all the world that such things were of no help whatever. The song of the Sirens could pierce through everything, and the longing of those they seduced would have broken far stronger bonds than chains and masts. But Ulysses did not think of that, although he had probably heard of it. He trusted absolutely to his handful of wax and his fathom of chain, and in innocent elation over his little stratagem sailed out to meet the Sirens.

Now the Sirens have a still more fatal weapon than their song, namely their silence. And through admittedly such a thing has never happened, still it is conceivable that some one might possibly have escaped from their singing; but from their silence certainly never. Against the feeling of having triumphed over them by one's own strength, and the consequent exaltation that bears down everything before it, no earthly powers could have remained intact.

And when Ulysses approached them the potent songstresses actually did not sing, whether because they thought that this enemy could be vanquished only by their silence, or because the look of bliss on the face of Ulysses, who was thinking of nothing but his wax and his chains, made them forget their singing.

But Ulysses, if one may so express it, did not hear their silence; he thought they were singing and that he alone did not hear them. For a fleeting moment he saw their throats rising and falling, their breasts lifting, their eyes filled with tears, their lips half-parted, but believed that these were accompaniments to the airs which died unheard around him. Soon, however, all this faded from his sight as he fixed his gaze on the distance; the Sirens literally vanished before his resolution; and at the very moment when they were nearest to him he knew of them no longer.

But they—lovelier than ever—stretched their necks and turned, let their cold hair flutter free in the wind, and forgetting everything clung with their claws to the rocks. They no longer had any desire to allure; all that they wanted was to hold as long as they could the radiance that fell from Ulysses' great eyes.

If the Sirens had possessed consciousness they would have been annihilated at that moment. But they remained as they had been; all that had happened was that Ulysses had escaped them.

A codicil to the foregoing has also been handed down. Ulysses, it is said, was so full of guile, was such a fox, that not even the goddess of fate could pierce his armour. Perhaps he had really noticed, although here the human understanding is beyond its depths, that the Sirens were silent, and opposed the afore-mention pretence to them and the gods merely as a sort of shield.

Franz Kafka (*The Great Wall of China,* trans. by Willa and Edwin Muir, New York, 1948)

THE BLOW

SOME were treacherous, as Halgerda the Fair. Three husbands she had, and was the death of every man of them. Her last lord was Gunnar of Lithend, the bravest and most peaceful of men. Once she did a mean thing, and he slapped her face. She never forgave him. At last enemies besieged him in his house. The doors were locked—all was quiet within. One of the enemies climbed up to a window slit, and Gunnar thrust him through with his lance. "Is Gunnar at home?" said the besiegers. "I know not—but his lance is," said the wounded man, and died with that last jest on his lips. For long Gunnar kept them at bay with his arrows, but at last one of them cut the arrow string. "Twist me a string with thy hair," he said to his wife, Halgerda, whose yellow hair was very long and beautiful. "Is it a matter of thy life or death?" she asked. "Ay," he said. "Then I remember that blow thou gavest me, and I will see thy death." So Gunnar died, overcome by numbers, and they killed Samr, his hound, but not before Samar had killed a man.

From *Essays in Little* (1891), by Andrew Lang

THE PATTERN ON THE CARPET

I READ over the lines again, and thinking over them I was reminded of Henry James' story, *The Pattern on the Carpet;* the notion of a man of letters who had written many books and was quite surprised to find that one of his admirers had failed to recognize that all these tales of his were variations on one theme; that a common pattern, like the pattern of an Eastern carpet, ran through them all. If I remember the novelist died suddenly, without revealing the nature of the pattern, and James ends very exquisitely, leaving us with the faithful admirer, who, we are to understand, is to pass the rest of his days in endeavouring to penetrate the mystery of this one design, latent in a whole shelf of books.

From *The London Adventure* (1924),
by Arthur Machen

THE STORY OF THE TWO KINGS
AND THE TWO LABYRINTHS

MEN worthy of credence (though Allah knows more) relate that in the early days there was a king of the islands of Babylon who gathered together all his architects and magicians and ordered them to construct a labyrinth so puzzling and subtle that the wisest men would never venture to enter it while those who did would lose themselves. This work constituted a scandal—for confusion and wonder are workings proper to God and not to man. With the passage of time a king of the Arabs visited the court, and the king of Babylon (to make mock of his visitor's simplicity) had him enter the labyrinth, where he wandered in shamed confusion until the fall of day. He called for divine help, and found the door. No word of complaint escaped his lips, but he told the king of Babylon that in Arabia he possessed a better labyrinth and that, if God so willed, he would show it to him some day. He went back then to Arabia, along with his captains and governors. Presently he returned and ravaged the kingdom of Babylon in such a thoroughgoing way that its forts were battered down, its people broken, and the king himself taken prisoner. He tied him on a swift camel and told him: "Oh king of time and of substance and cipher of the century! In Babylon you wanted to lose me in a bronze labyrinth of many stairs, doors, and walls. Now the All-Powerful has deemed it propitious for me to show you mine, where there are no stairs to climb, nor doors to force, nor weary galleries to wander, nor walls to block your way."

Thereupon he had him unbound and abandoned in the middle of the desert, where the Babylonian died of hunger and thirst. Glory be to Him who does not die.

From *The Land of Midian Revisited* (1879), by R. F. Burton

THE CONFESSION

In the spring of 1232, near Avignon, the knight Gontran D'Orville treasonably killed the hated Count Geoffroy, lord of the manor. He immediately confessed that he had thus avenged an offense: his wife had deceived him with the count.

They sentenced him to die by beheading, and ten minutes before the execution he was allowed to receive his wife in his cell.

"Why did you lie?" asked Giselle D'Orville. "Why have you disgraced me?"

"Because I am weak," replied her husband. "This way they will merely cut off my head. If I had confessed that I killed him because he was a tyrant, they would have tortured me first."

Manuel Peyrou

ANOTHER VERSION OF FAUST

DURING those years, the Podestá company toured the province of Buenos Aires, performing plays on *gaucho* themes. The first performance given in almost every town was a representation of *Juan Moreira,* but, on coming to the town of San Nicolás, they decided that it would be in good taste to do *Hormiga Negra,* the Black Ant. It is perhaps unnecessary to recall that the eponym had been in his youth the most famous swindler in these lands.

On the eve of the performance, a rather short man advanced in years and dressed in careful poverty presented himself in the field tent. "People are saying," he began, "that one of you is going to appear on Sunday in front of everybody and say he is Black Ant. I warn you that no one will be deceived, because I am Black Ant and everyone knows me."

The Podestá brothers waited upon him with that deference which is characteristic of them and they strove to make him understand that the theatrical piece in question constituted the most ingenious and idealistic homage to his legendary figure. It was all in vain, even though they ordered glasses of gin brought them on a tray from the hotel. The man, unshakeable in his decision, made it clear that no one had ever failed to pay him due respect, and that if anyone now put in an appearance claiming that he was Black Ant, he, old and all, would deal with him.

There was no avoiding the evidence! On Sunday, at the

hour announced, the Podestá company were representing *Juan Moreira* . . .

Fra Diavolo, "Vistazos críticos a los orígenes de nuestro teatro," *Caras y Caretas,* 1911

THE TREASURE

My brother hammered again, almost indignantly, on the resonant wall. He hammered one more time and there was the sound of an underground thunderclap. Little lines of sudden cracks appeared drawn on the wall and then, as if the hammer had hit upon the keystone, uneven blocks of wall came away and a hollow opening, dark and dust-filled, opened up before us. At first we perceived what seemed a shadow within the obscurity, a blacker area within the darkness. Avidly my brother began enlarging the hollow, and brought up the lamp. It was then that we saw him, standing erect, rigid, majestic. We could see, for an instant, his opulent brocade vestments, the glitter of his jewels, the clustered bouquet of bones around a gilt cross, his dried-earth skull supporting a tall mitre. He grew even larger with the light which my brother brought closer and then, dizzily, silently, the pulverized figure of the bishop toppled over. The bones were already dust, the mitre and the cope were dust. The jewels, heavy, ominous, eternal, were ours.

It suffices me now to say that the treasure trove—which we sold patiently and well—consisted of various episcopal rings, eight admirably jeweled monstrances, some heavy ciboria, crucifixes, and a late-Peruvian leather chest full of ancient coins and large gold medals.

Later, even I do not understand why we were in such a hurry to separate. I know the subsequent history of my brother's moves because he, brusque and bored, told it to me not long ago. He had begun, cautiously enough, husbanding his share of the money; then, almost without any intention on his part, it began to multiply. He grew very rich, married, had children, became even richer, reached the heights. Later, inexorably if gradually, he saw his fortune disappear and, from what I guessed, found the pleasure he formerly got from accumulating money also evanesce. He ended by not having a cent. And now he was indifferent to it all.

I, on the other hand, began by spending my part. I don't recall whether I have said that I am—or thought I was—a painter, and that at the time we discovered the secret niche I was beginning to draw at the academy in my own old city. It was natural, then, that I should devote the money to furthering my vocation. I went on a long trip to Europe and zealously sought the artist who should be my master. From Paris I went on to Venice, from Venice to Madrid. And there I stayed for more than twelve years. It was there I found the authentic Master, and I worked and lived and spent the years at his side. And I made progress. Secretly, for secrecy was his method, he transmitted his art to me. I learned his technique and his concept of reality; I saw the colors he saw, my hand moved with his pulse-beat. The Maestro taught me all he knew and perhaps more than he knew; sometimes I thought that the ideas he transmitted, in his superb way, were concepts he had just finished inventing. Nevertheless, the day arrived when he considered my apprenticeship completed; sorrowfully, I had to part from the Master and go my own way.

It was only a few months after my return that, one interminable night, I began to feel the obscure uncertainty that perhaps after all I was not a good painter. I had known, but without interest, other painters; I had seen, with disdain, other paintings. And now, suddenly, a restless uneasiness took possession of me. In profound mortification, with a confusion aggravated by inner distrust, I determined to spread my canvases to the public gaze. This was a course of action my Master had not authorized when we parted. In this state, I exhibited my work. As a result, it was said by someone that my painting was incomprehensible; the majority found it trivial. I soon realized that it was worthless, that I was not an artist at all. Of course I wrote my Master once, and then once again; I had no word of or from him ever again.

Disconsolate, I wandered about the house, day after day, like a child or a prisoner. Endlessly I roamed through the vast halls and rooms, the infinite corridors. Someone belonging to the house asked me once if I wanted to visit the room whose walls we had breached one night, led there then by a chance story we had heard. Up on the sepulchral wall, in the depths of the limitless house, someone had hung, from superstition or in all innocence, a portrait which, I was told, belonged to the immured bishop. It had been found, I was assured, shortly after my departure for Europe.

It was night when I went to see the painting and I had to use a lantern. I recall raising the lamp carefully before the rough wall and seeing the portrait illuminated in all its vastness. It was as if the lost scene were reproduced: I saw the same gilt cape, the same tall mitre. Only, in the portrait everything struck me, ironically, as more real. I stared then at something I could not recall, something I had not known; then, and not until that moment, I discovered that the Bishop had the face of my Master, that he was my Master.

Marcel Tamayo (Buenos Aires, July 1953)

93

THE GREATER TORMENT

THE demons told me that there is a hell for the sentimental and the pedantic. There they are abandoned in an interminable palace, more empty than full, and windowless. The damned walk about, as if searching for something, and, as we might expect, they soon begin to say that the greater torment consists in not participating in the vision of God, that moral suffering is worse than physical suffering, etcetera. Thereupon the demons hurl them into the sea of fire, from whence no one will ever save them.

The False Swedenborg, *Dreams* (1873)

THEOLOGY

As you are not unaware, I am much traveled. This fact allows me to corroborate the assertion that a voyage is always more or less illusory, that there is nothing new under the sun, that everything is one and the same, etcetera, but also, paradoxically enough, to assert that there is no foundation for despairing of finding surprises and something new: in truth, the world is inexhaustible. As proof for what I say, it will suffice to recall the strange and wonderful belief I discovered in Asia Minor, in a country of herdsmen who wear sheepskins for clothing and who are heirs to the ancient kingdom of the Magi. These people believe in sleep. "At the instant of falling asleep," they told me, "one goes, according to one's deeds during the day, either to heaven or hell." If anyone were to argue, "I have never seen a sleeping man go anywhere; in my experience, they lie where they are, until someone awakens them," they would then retort, "Your insistence in believing in nothing has led you to forget your own nights, for who has not known agreeable dreams and frightful ones? And thus you confuse sleep with death. Everyone is witness to the fact that there is another life for the dreamer; quite different is the evidence for the dead: they remain, turning to dust."

H. Garro, *Tout lou Mond,* Oloron-Saint-Marie (1918)

THE MAGNET

SPEAKING of Free Will as an illusion and of Destiny as inescapable, he [Wilde] improvised in this manner:

"Once upon a time there was a magnet, and in its close neighbourhood lived some steel filings. One day two or three little filings felt a sudden desire to go and visit the magnet, and they began to talk of what a pleasant thing it would be to do. Other filings nearby overheard their conversation, and they, too, became infected with the same desire. Still others joined them, till at last all the filings began to discuss the matter, and more and more their vague desire grew into an impulse. 'Why not go to-day?' said some of them; but others were of the opinion that it would be better to wait till to-morrow. Meanwhile, without their having noticed it, they had been involuntarily moving nearer to the magnet, which lay there quite still, apparently taking no heed of them. And so they went on discussing, all the time insensibly drawing nearer to their neighbour; and the more they talked, the more they felt the impulse growing stronger, till the more impatient ones declared that they would go that day, whatever the rest did. Some were heard to say it was their duty to visit the magnet, and that they ought to have gone long ago. And, while they talked, they moved always nearer and nearer, without realising that they had moved. Then, at last, the impatient ones prevailed, and, with one irresistible impulse, the whole body cried out, 'There is no use waiting. We will go to-day. We will go now. We will go at once.' And then in one unanimous mass they swept along, and in another moment were clinging fast to the magnet on every side. Then the magnet smiled—for the steel filings had no doubt at all but that they were paying that visit of their own free will."

From Chapter 13 of *The Life of Oscar Wilde*, by Hesketh Pearson (London, 1946–1954)

THE INEXTINGUISHABLE RACE

In that city everything was perfect and petite: the houses, the furniture, the tools, the shops, the gardens. I attempted to ascertain what sophisticated race of pygmies lived there. A hollow-eyed boy supplied the answer.

"It's we who do the work. Our parents, partly from egotism and self-indulgence, partly in order to please us and give us the pleasure of the work, established our present manner of living economically and agreeably. While they stay at home sitting in their houses, playing cards or music, reading or talking, loving or hating (for they are passionate people), we play the game of building and cleaning, of carpentry, harvesting, selling. Our work tools are of a size proportionate to our own size. And we manage to handle all our daily commitments with surprising facility. I must confess that, at the beginning, some of the animals, especially the tamed ones, did not respect us at all, because they knew we were children. But slowly, and by the use of a few tricks and lures on our part, they grew to respect us. The work we do is not difficult, but it is fatiguing. We often sweat like runaway horses. Sometimes we throw ourselves down on the ground and refuse to go on playing (we eat pasture grass then, or little lumps of earth, or are satisfied to lick the flagstones), but these whims last only a short time, they last 'as long as a summer storm,' as my girl-cousin says. Obviously not everything is an advantage for our parents. They, too, have their difficulties: they must enter their houses bent double, almost squatting, because the doors and the rooms themselves are tiny. The word *tiny* is always on their lips. The quantity of food they get is, according to my aunts, who are gluttonous, absolutely minimal. The cups and glasses from which they drink water do not prove sufficient for their thirst, and this may perhaps explain the recent wave of thievery as regards buckets and other hardware. Their clothes are all tight on them, for our machines are not adequate, will never be adequate for making larger clothes. Most adults, unless they have more than one bed for themselves, sleep bent double. They shiver with cold at night unless they manage to find a pile of blankets under which to hide, blankets which in the words of my own poor father, are more like handkerchiefs. At present people protest at the wedding cakes which nobody samples even out of politeness, at the wigs which do not cover the smallest bald spots, at the birdcages fit only for stuffed hummingbirds. I suspect that as a way of showing their malign displeasure, these same protesters almost never attend our ceremonies nor our theatrical or cinematographic performances. I should add that they do not fit in the seats in the theatres, and that the idea of sitting on the floor, in a public place, horrifies them. Nevertheless, certain people of middling stature, people without scruples (they are more numerous every day), occupy our places, behind our backs. We are trusting, but not absent-minded. Still, it took us a long time to root out the impostors. When adults are small, very small, they are like us; like us, that is, when we are tired: their faces are lined, they have swellings under their eyes, they speak in a vague **way,** mixing various languages. One day I was deceived by one of these creatures: I don't want to think of it. We can now detect these impostors more easily. We are on guard against them, so as to eject them from our circle. We are happy. I think we are happy.

"We are beset, it is true, by many uncertainties: there is a rumor going the rounds, for instance, that it is our fault that people do not grow, when they become adults, to their normal proportions, that is to say, to the disproportionate, the excessive measure which characterizes them. Certain of them retain the stature of a ten-year-old child; others, more fortunate, that of a seven-year-old. They try to be children and fail to understand that not everyone can be a child, merely because of a lack of a few inches. We, on the other hand, and according to statistics, are actually getting smaller without weakening and without ceasing to be what we are, without any attempt to deceive anyone.

"All this flatters our sense of pride, but it also disquiets us. My brother has already told me that he finds his carpenter's tools too heavy. A girl friend told me that her embroidery-needle seems as large as a sword to her. I myself find a certain amount of difficulty in handling a hatchet.

"We are not so much worried by the fact that our parents might occupy the role they have allowed us to play, for that is something we would never let them do, and we would smash our machines, destroy the electrical factories and piped-water installations, before handing them over; but we *are* preoccupied about posterity, the future of the race.

"Still, some among us assert that as we grow smaller in the course of time our view of the world will become more intimate, more human."

Silvina Ocampo

THE FACE OF DEATH

A YOUNG Persian gardener said to his Prince:

"Save me! I met Death this morning. He made a threatening face at me. Tonight, I would like, by some miracle, to be in Ispahan."

The bountiful Prince lends him his horses. That afternoon, the Prince encounters Death, and asks:

"Why did you make a threatening face at our gardener this morning?"

"It wasn't a threatening face," comes the reply, "but a surprised face. For I met him this morning far from Ispahan, and it is in Ispahan that I must take him tonight."

From *Le Grand Écart*, by Jean Cocteau

FAITH, HALF-FAITH, AND
NO FAITH AT ALL

In the ancient days there went three men upon pilgrimage; one was a priest, and one was a virtuous person, and the third was an old rover with his axe.

As they went, the priest spoke about the grounds of faith.

"We find the proofs of our religion in the works of nature," said he, and beat his breast.

"That is true," said the virtuous person.

"The peacock has a scrannel voice," said the priest, "as has been laid down always in our books. How cheering!" he cried, in a voice like one that wept. "How comforting!"

"I require no such proofs," said the virtuous person.

"Then you have no reasonable faith," said the priest.

"Great is the right, and shall prevail!" cried the virtuous person. "There is loyalty in my soul; be sure, there is loyalty in the mind of Odin."

"These are but playings upon words," returned the priest. "A sackful of such trash is nothing to the peacock."

Just then they passed a country farm where there was a peacock seated on a rail, and the bird opened its mouth and sang with the voice of a nightingale.

"Where are you now?" asked the virtuous person. "And yet this shakes not me! Great is the truth and shall prevail!"

"The devil fly away with that peacock!" said the priest; and he was downcast for a mile or two.

But presently they came to a shrine, where a Fakeer performed miracles.

"Ah!" said the priest, "here are the true grounds of faith. The peacock was but an adminicle. This is the base of our religion." And he beat upon his breast and groaned like one with colic.

"Now to me," said the virtuous person, "all this is as little to the purpose as the peacock. I believe because I see the right is great and must prevail; and this Fakeer might carry on with his conjuring tricks till doomsday, and it would not play bluff upon a man like me."

Now at this the Fakeer was so much incensed that his hand trembled; and lo! in the midst of a miracle, the cards fell from up his sleeve.

"Where are you now?" asked the virtuous person. "And yet it shakes not me!"

"The devil fly away with the Fakeer!" cried the priest. "I really do not see the good of going on with this pilgrimage."

"Cheer up!" cried the virtuous person. "Great is the right and shall prevail!"

"If you are quite sure it will prevail?" says the priest.

"I pledge my word for that," said the virtuous person.

So the other began to go on again with a better heart.

At last one came running, and told them all was lost: that the powers of darkness had besieged the Heavenly Mansions, that Odin was to die, and evil triumph.

"I have been grossly deceived," cried the virtuous person.

"All is lost now," said the priest.

"I wonder if it is too late to make it up with the devil?" said the virtuous person.

"O, I hope not," said the priest. "And at any rate we can but try. But what are you doing with your axe?" says he to the rover.

"I am off to die with Odin," said the rover.

R. L. Stevenson

THE MIRACLE

A Yogi wanted to cross a river and had not the penny to pay the ferryman, so he walked across the river on his feet. Another Yogi hearing of this said the miracle was only worth the penny it would have cost to cross by ferry.

> W. Somerset Maugham, *A Writer's Notebook*
> (London, 1949–1951)

TWO CO-ETERNALS

As is well-known, God the father is not anterior to God the Son.
When the Son was created, the Father asked him:
"Do you know how I went about creating you?"
The Son answered:
"By imitating me."

Johannes Cambrencis, *Animadversiones*
(Lichfield, 1709)

106

SOCIAL SUCCESS

THE servant gave me my coat and hat, and in a glow of self-satisfaction I walked out into the night. "A delightful evening," I reflected, "the nicest kind of people. What I said about finance and philosophy impressed them; and how they laughed when I imitated a pig squealing."

But soon after, "God, it's awful," I muttered, "I wish I was dead."

Logan Pearsall Smith, *Trivia* (1918)

THE TRAIN

THE train was on its daily late-afternoon run, toward sundown.
But it was running behind schedule, as if waiting on the land-
scape.

I had set out to buy something my mother wanted. The in-
terval was a pleasant one, as if the rolling of the train's wheels
was a matter of caressing the lubricious and slippery rails. Once
aboard I had set about playing at hunting down my oldest
memories, the first memories of my life. The train dallied so,
that I soon detected a maternal odor in my memory: milk being
heated, alcohol being burned. Thus, until the first stop: Haedo.
Next, I recalled children's games I played. I was going into ado-
lescence when Ramos Mejía appeared before my eyes: I was
offered a shady, romantic street, and a girl ready for courting.
I was married right there, after meeting and visiting her parents
in the patio of her house, which was almost Andalusian in style.
We were coming out of the town's church when I heard the
bell: the train was beginning to move on. I made my farewells
and, since I am very fast, was able to catch the train. Soon I
found myself in Ciudadela where my efforts strove to burrow
into a past perhaps impossible to resurrect in memory.

The station-master, who was a friend of mine, came to tell me
to prepare myself for some good news, for my wife had sent a
telegram to that effect. I struggled to come up with some in-
fantile terror (for I had felt such terror right enough), from

before the memory of heated milk and alcohol. At this juncture we reached Liniers. There, at that station so abounding and rich in time present offered by the RR company, I was able to be overtaken by my wife who was bringing the twins dressed in homemade clothes. We got off and, in one of those gleaming shops Liniers boasts, we outfitted them in store clothes, elegant enough, and also bought them fine school-cases and books. We quickly found the same train on which we had been travelling and which had been long delayed while another train unloaded milk-containers. My wife, though, stayed behind at Liniers, while I remained on the train, enjoying the sight of my children, so elegant and robust as they talked of football and telling the jokes which youth thinks it has invented. But in Flores the inconceivable awaited me: a delay caused by a crash of railway cars and an accident at a crossing. Meanwhile, the station-master at Liniers, who knew me, had gotten in touch by telegraph with the station-master of Flores. He had bad news for me. My wife had died, and the funeral cortège would try to overtake the train detained in Flores. I alighted from the train in tribulation, unable to tell the children anything at all, since I had sent them on ahead toward Caballito, where their school was located.

With the help of some relatives and close friends we buried my wife in the cemetery at Flores, where a simple iron cross gives her name and marks the site of her invisible detention. When we returned to Flores town, we found that the train which had accompanied us through such happy and such sad events was still there. I said farewell at El Once to my in-laws and, with my mind on my poor orphaned children and my dead wife, I made my way like a somnambulist to the Insurance Company where I worked. But I could not find the place.

By asking the oldest people I could locate roundabout, I found out that the "Insurance Company" building had long ago been demolished. In its place stood a building twenty-five stories high. I was told that it was a Ministry building, where un-surance reigned, where insecurity infected everything from the jobs to the decrees. I got into an elevator, and once on the twenty-fifth floor, I ran furiously to the first window and threw myself out and down into the street. I fell in among the foliage of a full tree with branches and leaves like a cottony fig tree. The flesh of my body, which was about to shatter into pieces, dispersed into memories. The band of memories, together with my body, was delivered to my mother. "I'll bet you didn't remember what I sent you for," she said, as she jokingly feigned to threaten me. "You've the mind of a bird."

Santiago Dabove (1946)

A PROVOCATION PUNISHED

MODJALAID narrates that Noah passed a lion stretched out on the ground and gave it a kick as he went by; in doing so he hurt himself and was unable to sleep the whole night long. "My Lord," he cried out, "your dog hurt me!" God sent him the following revelation: "God reproves injustice, and you began it."

Ah'med el Qalyubi, *Kitab en Nanadir*

TALE

THE King commanded ("I condemn You to die, but to die as Xios and not as You!") that Xios be taken to an altogether different country. His name was to be changed, his features artistically mutilated. The people of the new country were to create a new past for him, a new family, talents very different to his own.

If he chanced to recall anything of his former life, they refuted him, told him he was mad, and so on . . .

They had prepared a family for him, a wife and children who said they were his.

In short, everything and everybody told him that he was who he was not.

Paul Valéry, *Histoires Brisées* (1950)

PRESTIGIEUX, SANS DOUTE

THE masked man was ascending the stairway. His footfalls resounded in the night: tick, tack, tick, tack.

Aguirre Acevedo, *Fantasmagorías* (1927)

THE UBIQUITOUS ONE, I

On leaving the city of Stravasti, the Buddha had to cross an extensive plain. From their various heavens, the gods threw him parasols to cover him from the sun. In order to avoid giving offense or slighting any of his benefactors, the Buddha courteously multiplied himself, and thus each one of the gods beheld a Buddha who walked along with his own parasol.

Moriz Winternitz, *Geschichte der indischen Literatur* (1920)

THE UBIQUITOUS ONE, II

A VERSION given by Sir William Jones would have it that a despondent Hindustani god, one afflicted by his celibacy, solicited of another god the loan of one of his 14,516 wives. The husband consented with these words: "Take the one you find unoccupied." The needy god went visiting each of the 14,516 palaces. In each one, the lady of the house was with her lord.

The latter had increased himself 14,515 times and each wife thought herself the only one to enjoy his favors.

Simon Pereyra, S.J., *Cuarenta años en el lecho del Ganges* (Goa, 1887)

THE OVERSIGHT

It is related:

Rabbi Elimelekh was supping with his disciples. The servant brought him a plate of soup. The Rabbi turned it over and the soup spilled all over the table. Young Mendel, who was to become Rabbi of Rimanov, exclaimed:

"Rabbi, what have you done? They will put us all in jail."

The other disciples smiled, and would have laughed openly, but the presence of the master held them back. The latter, however, did not smile. He nodded his head affirmatively and said to Mendel:

"Do not fear, my son."

It was learned some time later that on that same day an edict directed against all the Jews in the country had been presented to the Emperor for his signature. The Emperor had taken up his pen a number of times, but something always interrupted him. Finally he signed. He stretched his hand out toward the sand-box to dry the ink, but instead he picked up the ink-well by mistake and spilled it over the paper. Whereupon he tore it up—and ordered they never bring it to him again.

Martin Buber

THE SECT OF THE WHITE LOTUS

ONCE there was a man who belonged to the sect of the White Lotus. And many, wishing to dominate the dark arts, accepted him as Master.

One day the necromancer prepared to set out. In his vestibule he placed a bowl covered by another bowl, and directed his disciples to watch over it. He told them not to uncover the bowl or to look inside.

He had scarcely gone, when they lifted the top bowl and saw that the bottom one contained pure water and in the water a small straw boat rigged with masts and sails. Surprised, they gave the boat a push with their fingers. It turned over. Quickly they righted it and put back the top bowl.

The necromancer at once appeared and said:

"Why have you disobeyed me?"

The disciples stood up and denied that they had. The necromancer declared:

"My ship went down in the Yellow Sea. How dare you deceive me?"

One afternoon he lit a small candle in the corner of his courtyard. He ordered his disciples to guard it from the wind. The second watch came and went, and the necromancer had not returned. Weary and full of sleep, the disciples lay down and dozed. The next day they found the candle out. They lit it again.

The necromancer at once appeared and said:

"Why have you disobeyed me?"

The disciples denied it:

"Truly, we have not slept. How could the candle go out?"

The necromancer told them:

"I wandered lost for fifteen leagues in the darkness of the Tibetan desert and now you try to deceive me."

This time the disciples were stricken with terror.

Richard Wilhelm, *Chinesische Volksmärchen* (1924)

PROTECTION THROUGH THE BOOK

THE learned Wu, from Ch'iang Ling, had insulted the necromancer Chang Ch'i Shen. Convinced that the latter would wreak vengeance, Wu spent the night awake, reading, by the light of a lamp, in the sacred Book of Transformations. Suddenly a clap of wind was heard surrounding the house and a warrior appeared in the doorway threatening him with a lance. Wu knocked him down with his book. When he bent over to look at him, he found he was no more than a figure cut out of paper. Wu put him away between the leaves of his book. Shortly afterwards, two small malign spirits, black-faced and brandishing axes, entered the room. Wu knocked them down with his book, and they too turned out to be paper figures. Wu put them away as he had the others. At midnight a wailing woman in tears knocked at the door.

"I am Chang's wife," she declared. "My husband and my two sons came here to attack you and you have put them away in your book. I beg you to let them go."

"Neither your husband nor your sons are in my book," Wu replied. "I have only these paper figures."

"Their souls are in those figures," said the woman. "If they have not returned by dawn, their bodies, which lie at home, will not be able to revive."

"Damnable conjurers!" yelled Wu. "What mercy can they

expect? I do not propose to set them at liberty. Because I feel sorry for you, I will give you back one of your sons, but do not ask for more."

Wu handed her one of the black-faced paper-figures.

The next day, he learned that the necromancer and his elder son had died the night before.

G. Willoughby-Meade, *Chinese Ghouls and Goblins* (1928)

THE MEETING

BROUGHT up on a hatred of Rome and educated to destroy it, the two brothers Hannibal and Hasdrubal invaded Italy, one from the south, the other from the north. The brothers did not see each other for eleven years; they planned to meet in Rome, on the day of victory. But the Consul Gaius Claudius Nero defeated Hasdrubal on the banks of the River Metaurus. He ordered that Hasdrubal's head be cut off and that it be thrown into Hannibal's camp. Thus did Hannibal learn that Hasdrubal had been vanquished.

Louis Prolat, *La Tarif de Marseille* (1869)

THE WATER ON THE ISLAND

On account of the singular character of the water, we refused to taste it, supposing it to be polluted . . . I am at a loss to give a distinct idea of the nature of this liquid, and cannot do so without many words. Although it flowed with rapidity in all declivities where common water would do so, yet never, except when falling in a cascade, had it the customary appearance of *limpidity* . . . At first sight, and especially in cases where little declivity was found, it bore resemblance, as regards consistency, to a thick infusion of gum arabic in common water. But this was only the least remarkable of its extraordinary qualities. It was *not* colorless, nor was it of any one uniform color—presenting to the eye, as it flowed, every possible shade of purple, like the hues of a changeable silk . . . Upon collecting a basinful, and allowing it to settle thoroughly, we perceived that the whole mass of liquid was made up of a number of distinct veins, each of a distinct hue; that these veins did not commingle . . . Upon passing the blade of a knife athwart the veins, the water closed over it immediately, as with us, and also, in withdrawing it, all traces of the passage of the knife were instantly obliterated. If, however, the blade was passed down accurately between the two veins, a perfect separation was effected, which the power of cohesion did not immediately rectify.

From the *Narrative of A. Gordon Pym,* Edgar Allan Poe (The Works of E. A. Poe, New York, 1900)

ON EXACTITUDE IN SCIENCE

. . . In that Empire, the Art of Cartography achieved such Per-
fection that the Map of one single Province occupied the whole
of a City, and the Map of the Empire, the whole of a Province.
In time, those Disproportionate Maps failed to satisfy and the
Schools of Cartography sketched a Map of the Empire which
was of the size of the Empire and coincided at every point with
it. Less Addicted to the Study of Cartography, the Following
Generations comprehended that this dilated Map was Useless
and, not without Impiety, delivered it to the Inclemencies of the
Sun and of the Winters. In the Western Deserts there remain
piecemeal Ruins of the Map, inhabited by Animals and Beggars.
In the entire rest of the Country there is no vestige left of the
Geographical Disciplines.

Suárez Miranda, *Viajes de Varones Prudentes,*
libro cuarto, cap. XIV (Lérida, 1658)

THE DEDICATED STUDENT

"FROM the age of seven I felt the impulse to draw the forms of things. Approaching fifty, I exhibited a collection of drawings; but nothing executed before my seventies satisfies me. Only at seventy-three was I able to intuit, even if only approximately, the true form and nature of birds, fish, and plants. Consequently, when I am eighty I will have made great progress; at ninety I shall have penetrated to the essence of all things; at one hundred I shall certainly have ascended to a higher, indescribable state, and if I reach one hundred and ten, everything, each point and each line, will live. I invite those who live as long as I do to verify whether or not I keep these promises."

Written at the age of seventy-five by me, formerly Hokusai, now called Huakivo-Royi, the old man mad for drawing.*

* Hokusai died at the age of 89.

Adler-Revon, *Japanische Literatur*

THE VICISSITUDES OF CONSOLATION

THIS all must have happened some one thousand seven hundred years before the Classical period, in the kingdom of Hsia, which extended as far as the bend in the Yellow River. The populace was proud of its religion: it had freed itself of gullibility, and of vulgar belief in sea-serpents, lions, gods, witches, the evil eye, all of which it considered common and crude, and it had not fallen into incredulous materialism either. They maintained one single article of faith, but in regard to that one article no one doubted. No one doubted, in short, that in addition to his own head, everyone boasted a supposed or assumed one; that is to say (who ignores our meaning?), a supposed head; and that in addition to the trunk of his body, everyone disposed of a supposed trunk, and thus with one's arms, one's legs, and other parts of the body, however small they might be. No one doubted this until a heretic made his appearance, a heretic whom the Portuguese chronicles denominate as *o Litrado,* the Lettered One, "with only one face," and whom the Jesuit compilations call "the Lettered One without a face." In his preaching, this man ran into difficulties and obstacles. When he attempted to explain that no cripple taking advantage of his supposed leg did without crutches, he was told that such cases of debilitated faith were, disgracefully and unfortunately, frequent enough, but that they proved nothing against the true religion. And, in any case, they argued (with a slight change of tone), asking why anyone should throw away a belief which was so little burdensome and which, in moments of sadness and depression (which can always be counted upon), could provide comfort and consolation?

T. M. Chang, *A Grove of Leisure*
(Shanghai, 1882)

THE TRUTH ABOUT SANCHO PANZA

WITHOUT making any boast of it Sancho Panza succeeded in the course of years, by devouring a great number of romances of chivalry and adventure in the evening and night hours, in so diverting from him his demon, whom he later called Don Quixote, that his demon thereupon set out in perfect freedom on the maddest exploits, which however, for the lack of a pre-ordained object, which should have been Sancho Panza himself, harmed nobody. A free man, Sancho Panza philosophically followed Don Quixote on his crusades, perhaps out of a sense of responsibility, and had of them a great and edifying entertainment to the end of his days.

Franz Kafka

SALVATION

THIS is a story out of past times and kingdoms. A sculptor was walking in the gardens of the palace in the company of a tyrant. Beyond and behind the Labyrinth for Illustrious Foreigners, at the far edge of the Grove dedicated to Decapitated Philosophers, the sculptor presented the tyrant with his latest work: a water-nymph as fountain. While he grew prolix with technical explanations and expanded in the intoxication of triumph, the artist began to notice a menacing shadow crossing the handsome face of his protector. He fathomed the cause. "How can a person of such indifferent quality," the tyrant was surely thinking, "do what I, the master of nations, cannot do?" At that moment a bird, which had settled to drink at the fountain, flew off with a flutter of wings in the air, and the sculptor thought of the idea which would save him. "No matter how insignificant they may be," he said aloud, indicating the bird, "we must recognize that they fly better than we."

Adolfo Bioy Casares

IN INSOMNIA

THE man goes to bed early. He cannot go to sleep. He turns over in his bed, logically enough. He twists the sheets. He lights a cigar. He reads a bit. He puts out the light again. But he cannot induce sleep. At three in the morning he gets up. He awakens his friend next door and confides in him; he cannot sleep. He asks for advice. The friend advises him to take a walk and perhaps tire himself out; and then to drink a cup of linden-tea and turn off the light. He does all these things but he does not manage to sleep. Again he gets up. This time he goes to see the doctor. As always happens the doctor talks a good deal, but the man still does not go to sleep. At six in the morning he loads a revolver and blows out his brains. The man is dead but he has not been able to get any sleep. Insomnia is a very persistent thing.

Virgilio Piñera (1946)

DISTRACTED

A HUNTER, by way of stampeding the game, set fire to the woods around them. Of a sudden, he saw a man emerging from a rock.

The man calmly walked through the fire. The hunter ran after him.

"Tell me, there. How do you manage to go through rock?"

"Rock? What do you mean by that?"

"I also saw you walk through fire!"

"Fire? What do you mean by fire?"

That perfect Taoist, totally effaced, saw no difference between things.

Henri Michaux, *Un barbare en Asie*

THE EGYPTIAN TEMPTATION

For several years before he adopted the trade of a bookseller, which was that of his father, he pursued no other occupation than that of performing in the religious ceremonies called "zikrs"; which consist in the repetition of the name and attributes, &c., of God, by a number of persons, in chorus; and in such performances he is still often employed. He was then a member of the order of the Saadeeyeh darweeshes, who are particularly famous for devouring live serpents; and he is said to have been one of the serpent-eaters: but he did not confine himself to food so easily digested. One night, during a meeting of a party of darweeshes of his order, at which their Sheykh was present, my friend became affected with religious frenzy, seized a tall glass shade which surrounded a candle placed on the floor, and ate a large portion of it. The Sheykh and the other darweeshes, looking at him with astonishment, upbraided him with having broken the institutes of his order; since the eating of glass was not among the miracles which they were allowed to perform; and they immediately expelled him. He then entered the order of the Ahmedeeyeh; and as they, likewise, never ate glass, he determined not to do so again. However, soon after, at a meeting of some brethren of this order, when several Saadeeyeh also were present, he again was seized with frenzy, and, jumping up to a chandelier, caught hold of one of the small glass lamps attached to it,

131

and devoured about half of it, swallowing also the oil and water which it contained. He was conducted before his Sheykh, to be tried for this offense; but on his taking an oath never to eat glass again, he was neither punished nor expelled from the order. Notwithstanding this oath, he soon again gratified his propensity to eat a glass lamp; and a brother-darweesh, who was present, attempted to do the same; but a large fragment stuck between the tongue and palate of this rash person; and my friend had great trouble to extract it.

> Edward William Lane, *Manners and Customs of the Modern Egyptians* (1836), Author's Preface

RETROSPECTIVE

At the time of the Flood, they ordered a Noah's Ark so that the animals would not drown.

> Clemente Sosa, *Informe sobre la conducción de haciendas en pie en balsas entre Villa Constitución y Campana* (Campana, 1913)

THE ACCUSED

IT is related:

The Emperor at Vienna proclaimed an edict which would aggravate the already wretched condition of the Jews of Galicia. In those years, there lived, in the work-studio of Rabbi Elimelekh, a serious student called Feivel. One night Feivel got up, went to the Rabbi's room, and told him:

"Master, I would like to bring a suit against God."

His own words struck him with terror when he heard them.

The Rabbi answered:

"Good enough, but the court does not meet at night."

The following day, two masters arrived in Lizhensk: Israel of Koznitz and Jacob Yitzhak from Lublin, and they stopped at Rabbi Elimelekh's house. After a collation the Rabbi summoned Feivel and told him:

"Now explain your suit to us."

"I no longer have the strength to do so," stuttered Feivel.

"I shall give you the strength," said the Rabbi.

Feivel began to speak:

"Why do they keep us in servitude in this Empire? Did not God say in the Torah: 'The children of Israel are my servants'? He has sent us into foreign lands, but he should set us free, so that we may serve Him."

To this Rabbi Elimelekh answered:

"Now the plaintiff and defendant should withdraw from the court, as the law requires, to prevent exercising any influence upon the judges. Retire, therefore, Rabbi Feivel. We cannot, Lord of the world, ask You to leave, for your glory fills the world, and without your presence we could not live a single moment. But neither, Lord, shall we let you influence us."

The three deliberated in silence and with their eyes closed. At nightfall they summoned Feivel and gave him their decision. His claim was a just one. At that same hour the Emperor cancelled his edict.

Martin Buber

THE SPECTATOR

DON JUAN: Whose funeral is that going by?
STATUE: Your own. Why?
DON JUAN: Dead! Me?
STATUE: The Captain killed thee
      As you came from your house to lie.

José Zorrilla, *Don Juan Tenorio,* (1844),
Act III, Scene 2

PERILS OF AN EXCESS OF PIETY

ONE day when Abu Nonas was visiting a friend, the roof began to creak. "What's that?" he asked. "Do not fear, it is merely the roof praising the Lord." As soon as he heard these words, Abu Nonas quit the house. "Where are you going?" his friend called after him. "I am afraid that its devotion will increase," answered Abu Nonas, "and that it will prostrate itself with me inside."

Nozhat el Djallas

CONCLUSION FOR A FANTASY

"How strange!" said the girl, advancing warily. "What a heavy door!" As she spoke she touched it, and it suddenly banged shut.

"My God!" exclaimed the man. "I don't think there's a latch or bolt on the inside here. Why, you've locked both of us up in here."

"Both of us, no. Only one of us," said the girl, as she passed through the door and disappeared.

I. A. Ireland, *Visitations* (1919)

FOUR REFLECTIONS

LEOPARDS break into the temple and drink the sacrificial chalices dry; this occurs repeatedly, again and again: finally it can be reckoned upon beforehand and becomes a part of the ceremony.

The crows maintain that a single crow could destroy the heavens. Doubtless that is so, but it proves nothing against the heavens, for the heavens signify simply: the impossibility of crows.

The hunting dogs are playing in the courtyard, but the hare will not escape them, no matter how fast it may be flying already through the woods.

The choice was put to them whether they would like to be kings or king's couriers. Like children they all wanted to be couriers. So now there are a great many couriers, they post through the world, and, as there are no kings left, shout to each other their meaningless and obsolete messages. They would gladly put an end to their wretched lives, but they dare not because of their oath of service.

Franz Kafka, "Reflections on Sin, Pain, Hope and the True Way" (in *The Great Wall of China*, trans. by W. and E. Muir, New York, 1948)

STORY WITH FOXES

WANG saw two foxes standing on their hind legs and leaning against a tree. One of them held a sheet of paper in its hand, and the pair laughed as if sharing a joke.

He tried frightening them away. But they stood their ground; and so he shot against the one holding the paper; he wounded the fox in the eye, and then he went and picked up the paper. In the inn later, he recounted his adventure to the other guests. While he was speaking, a gentleman entered, a gentleman with a wound in one eye. He listened to Wang's story with interest and asked to be shown the paper. Wang was in the course of showing it, when the innkeeper noticed that the newcomer had a tail. "It's a fox!" He exclaimed, and on the instant the gentleman turned into a fox and fled.

Repeatedly the foxes attempted to retrieve the paper, which was covered with unintelligible characters, but they failed. Wang got ready to return to his own home. On the road he met his entire family on the way to the capital. They explained that they were moving in compliance with his directions, and his mother showed him the letter in which he asked them to sell all their lands and property and join him in the capital. Wang examined the letter and saw that it was a sheet of blank paper: Though they no longer had a roof to give them shelter, Wang declared: "Let us return."

One day a younger brother, whom they had thought dead, appeared among them. He asked after the family in their misfortune, and Wang told him the whole story. "Ah!" said the brother, when Wang got to his encounter with the foxes, "there lies the root of all the trouble." Wang showed him the document. Grabbing it away from Wang, his brother quickly put it away. "At last I've gotten what I was looking for," he exclaimed and, turning himself into a fox, ran away.

Niu Chiao, *Ling kuai lu*
(ninth century)

JUST IN CASE

REDWALD [king of the East Saxons] had . . . been admitted to the Sacrament of the Christian faith in Kent, but in vain, for on his return home, he was seduced by his wife and certain perverse teachers, and turned back from the sincerity of the faith; . . . and in the same temple he had an altar to sacrifice to Christ, and another small one to offer victims to devils.*

> The Venerable Bede, *The Ecclesiastical History of the English Nation,* II, 15 (trans. by John Stevens and Lionel Jane, London, 1944)

* Bede calls the ancient Germanic divinities "devils." And cf. the Introduction by V. D. Scudder, *op. cit.:* ". . . the small altar to Odin erected by King Redwald in a Christian Church."

142

ODIN

One night, it is related, a man appeared at the court of Olaf Tryggvason, who had converted to the new faith. The man was old, enveloped in a dark cape, and the brim of his hat hung over his eyes. The King asked him if he knew how to do anything; the stranger answered that he knew how to play the harp and tell stories. He played ancient airs on the harp, spoke of Gudrun and Gunnar, and, finally, told of the birth of Odin. He related that three fates had appeared: the first two promised great happiness, but the third angrily announced: "The child will not live longer than the candle burning at his side." The parents snuffed the candle, then, so that Odin might not die. Olaf Tryggvason doubted the story; the stranger repeated that it was a true one; he took out the candle and lit it. While they watched it burn, the man said it was late and he must leave. When the candle had burnt itself out, they went to look for him. A few steps from the King's house, Odin lay dead.

Jorge Luis Borges and Delia Ingenieros,
Antiguas literaturas germánicas (1951)

AUREA MEDIOCRITAS

MALHERBE was not any too certain there was another life, and he used to say, whenever they spoke to him of heaven and hell: "I have lived like everyone else, I want to die like everyone else, I want to go where everyone else goes."

Tallemant des Réaux, *Les Historiettes,* XXIX